TALES OF THE UNREMEMBERED

Rosi MorganBarry

Rosi MorganBarry

Kingdom Publishers

www.kingdompublishers.co.uk

Tales of the Unremembered
Stories of those who shared the life and times of Jesus
Copyright© Rosi Morgan-Barry

All rights reserved.

No part of this book may be reproduced in any form by photocopying or any electronic or mechanical means, including information storage or retrieval systems, without permission in writing from both the copyright owner and the publisher of the book. The right of Rosi Morgan-Barry to be identified as the author of this work has been asserted by him in accordance with the Copyright, Designs and Patents Act 1988 and any subsequent amendments thereto. A catalogue record for this book is available from the British Library.

All Scripture Quotations have been taken from the New International Version and the King James Version of the Bible.

ISBN: 978-1-913247-94-2

1st Edition by Kingdom Publishers
Kingdom Publishers
London, UK.

You can purchase copies of this book from any leading bookstore or email contact@kingdompublishers.co.uk

DEDICATION

In memory of my adoptive parents, George and Elsie Sage, who led me to faith, with love and understanding.

Contents

TALES OF THE UNREMEMBERE

Introduction   5

Section 1 - *THE EARLY YEARS*   7

   Chapter 1 - *THE JOURNEY*   8

   Chapter 2 - *SYNAGOGUE SCHOOL*   14

   Chapter 3 - *LITTLE SISTER*   19

   Chapter 4 - *THE TEMPLE TRADER*   24

Section 2 - *THE MINISTRY*   28

   Chapter 5 - *THE PIG FARMER*   29

   Chapter 6 - *A HUNGRY BOY*   34

   Chapter 7 - *ONE OF SEVENTY-TWO*   39

   Chapter 8 - *HEALING AT THE POOL*   44

Section 3 - *TOWARDS JERUSALEM*   51

   Chapter 9 - *PHILIP AND THE DONKEY*   52

   Chapter 10 - *THE NEW CLOAK*   58

   Chapter 11 - *THE BOY WHO SHOUTED TO STONES*   63

   Chapter 12 - *THE PERFUME SELLER*   68

   Chapter 13 - *THE TEMPLE TRADER - AGAIN*   73

   Chapter 14 - *THE TALE OF A SOLDIER*   77

   Chapter 15 - *AN ORDINARY WOMAN*   82

   Chapter 16 - *FAMILY-BAR-JOSEPH*   86

TALES OF THE UNREMEMBERE
INTRODUCTION

These are stories of unknown people – those who were in Israel during the momentous years when Jesus was born, grew up, taught and healed, suffered and died and rose again.

They are the people who knew his family; those who were in the crowds; those who came, listened, watched, went home, told others.

Some continued to doubt; some would not even try to understand this man Jesus.

Many could not accept his message, refused to acknowledge his new spiritual direction.

Many went away wondering what he was talking about.

But many others did become believers, went on to tell their stories and spread the gospel.

They are unremembered, because we did not know who they were.

They are unnamed and unknown, but who exist in our imaginations.

These stories are for those whose work is to tell in our own time to young and old, what Jesus came to teach by his healing and his life.

Let their stories speak to us, for in them we may find our own tales to tell.

The Early Years:
    The Journey
    At Synagogue School
    Little Sister
    The Temple Trader

The Ministry:
    The Pig Farmer
    A Hungry Boy
    One of Seventy-two
    Healing at the Pool

Towards Jerusalem:
    Philip and the Donkey
    The New Cloak
    The Boy who Shouted to Stones
    The Perfume Seller

The End, the Beginning:
    The Temple Trader - again
    Tale of a Soldier
    An Ordinary Woman
    Family Bar-Joseph

Section 1
THE EARLY YEARS

Chapter 1
THE JOURNEY

An angel of the Lord appeared in a dream to Joseph and said: 'Herod will be looking for the child to kill him. So get up, take the child and his mother and escape to Egypt'…… (Herod) was furious, and gave orders to kill all the boys in Bethlehem and its neighbourhood who were two years old and younger.
Matthew 2: 13, 16

We didn't belong anywhere, Hapet and I. He was Egyptian; I was a Jew, a daughter of Abraham. I could trace my ancestry back to the tribe of Benjamin. An unusual alliance you might think, but among those of us who lived and worked in Egypt, I was not the only Jewish girl to fall in love with a handsome Egyptian. But to marry one? Our Rabbi, who is strict in such matters, has declared that such a thing cannot be allowed, and therefore since my marriage to Hapet I can no longer be considered to belong to my tribe. Or to any tribe. According to him, I am without citizenship or status in Israel. My father acknowledges this in public, but in secret, both he and my mother disagree, and in secret we visit my brother and his family in Bethlehem whenever Hapet's work takes us into Judah.

There are many Jewish families such as ours in Egypt and we are accepted into Egyptian society. My father works in the government office as a tax collector, and he trained Hapet for the work. It's a good job, but has its drawbacks, one of them being that no-one likes paying their taxes, particularly to our Roman overlords, and many people believe that all tax collectors are thieves and rogues. Both my father and my husband are honest tax men – there are quite a few of them – and have never cheated anyone. They demand what is owing, neither more nor less, and pay their collected dues into the tax office.

The census, called by Emperor Augustus involved a huge amount of work for the various offices throughout the Empire, and much travelling for Hapet. It was one of our journeys back to Egypt from Bethlehem that remains with me. We try never to travel alone, and to link up with other groups of merchants, or families travelling the same way. On this particular journey we joined a young family with a son who was about a year or two younger than my son Modi, who was five. The two lads immediately made friends and chatted together in a childish language that was a mix of Aramaic and Egyptian, and which they each seemed to understand perfectly. We grown-ups could not make head or tail of it, but it made us laugh and kept them happy. They were soon playing some kind of make-believe game, which involved Modi playing Pharaoh and little Jeshua being given the role of Moses.

Now there was a tale with two very different viewpoints! For us, the Jewish people, Moses was a hero and a patriarch; for Hapet and family, Moses' role in their history was one of the worst of times, and naturally, all Egyptian children are taught to think of him as a bringer of disasters. How the two little boys played this out was fascinating to us to watch. Joseph and Miriam, Jeshua's parents were as intrigued as we were to see Modi strutting about and Jeshua running after him and chatting away in their child-talk, tugging at his tunic as though to make him listen. Whether either of them understood what they were playing at that young age was something we found impossible to grasp.

But we soon had other things to worry us. From behind us we could hear the tramp of an army on the march; a cohort of Herod's soldiers. We travellers scattered to the sides of the road to let them pass by; had we not done so we would have been in danger of being trampled under their feet. I called the boys to me. But the captain came striding up, calling us all to 'Halt – in the name of King Herod'.

Miriam and Joseph remained close as he began to question us:

'Where were we from? Where were we going? Where did we live?'

Hapet answered for us all: he gave his name and work status; explained we had come from Jerusalem, where he had been helping to organise the census. I was surprised he said that.

True we had been in Jerusalem, but had actually come from Bethlehem, following a visit to my brother. Hapet, for some reason, seemed to include Miriam and Joseph as part of our family group, which they did not deny. The captain turned his attention to the boys who looked up at him bright-eyed.

'How old are they?'

I answered this time:

'Modi is five and Jesus three' – now why did I say that? I had no idea how old the child was! I then went on to introduce them:

'This is Modi' … but my son interrupted me.

'No' he said firmly, 'I'm Pharaoh, King of Egypt – and this is my son, Moses'.

The soldier was amused. He had, he said, sons of his own who took delight in playing such games. Nothing his older boy liked better than to play the king, and order the others to do his bidding! He called his cohort to attention and they went on their way, stopping to question others travelling ahead of us.

The boys returned to their game, pretending power beyond their small frames. Joseph and Miriam came with us to our home village, where Joseph found work as a carpenter. They stayed with us for a while and Joseph did some work in our house. It was good work, so it was easy to recommend him to others.

They went back to Judah after a few years. I shall miss them.

But a short while after that journey, when we visited my brother and his family again, I learned of the dreadful event in Bethlehem which had occurred a few days after our previous visit: how mad King Herod had ordered all boys of two years and younger to be killed. What reason could be given for such an act of cruelty? My brother and his wife had been appalled.

'Give thanks to the Lord that our boys were older, and that your Modi was five years old', my sister-in-law had said.

How old had little Jesus been when we travelled that journey with them? I wondered.

Chapter 2
SYNAGOGUE SCHOOL

*Jesus grew in both body and in wisdom,
gaining favour with God and men.
Luke 2: 52*

Me and Jesh, we was like brothers. Better 'n' brothers. We're the same age, nearly, him being a bit older 'n' me but not much. Anyway he's better 'n' me real brother who's lots older 'n' me an' thinks he can tell me what to do all the time. Jesh never does that. He always says:

'What d'you think?' or

'What about doing such 'n' such?' when we're off on adventures.

We've been together since before we both started first school at the House of the Book. Me dad's pottery business and Jesh's dad's carpentry business was next each other in the market place, and we'd often play there, where our dads could keep an eye on us when our mums were busy shopping.

He was good at school was Jesh. I remember our first day. Me mum said to walk with Jesh and not to run off anywhere, and not to eat my lunch before the Rabbi said we could, and to listen to everything and try and keep it in my head, 'cos that's how we learn. Me mum always said I couldn't keep nothing in me head an' I was always forgetting things.

'Don't know how you'll learn anything at school', she said.

Well, that first day I was so scared I forgot my lunch and had to run back for it. Jesh said he come with me, otherwise I'd be late 'cos I'd forget where I was going or something. We weren't late – not very late anyway. We slid in and sat down quick while the Rabbi was getting the scrolls out of the chest and when he turned round, there we was! Jesh just smiled up at him and he never said a word!

I hated school! I couldn't remember the words the Rabbi read out to us, which we had to say with him and then say on our own. They were the words of the stories: Moses and Joshua and Gideon and Elijah. They weren't too bad 'cos they had adventures – like Moses doing magic tricks before Pharaoh and both Moses and Joshua making the river pile up so's our people could cross, and Gideon with his bundle of wool, which wasn't wet when it should have been, and was wet when it shouldn't have been, and

Elijah calling down fire which licked up all the water. The Psalms weren't too bad either. But I couldn't remember the words of the Laws or what the prophets said.

Jesh helped me a lot. When we walked home, he'd recite the words and make them into a sort of tune, saying them line by line as we went along, which made them a bit easier for me to keep in me head. He'd make up funny stories too, to help me learn things. He never had any problem learning, but he never said what a ninny I was. Like me brother used to do.

After a bit we had to learn to write. We copied out letters on our wax tablets and mine never looked quite right. I was always having to rub them out and do them again. But the worst bit was having to learn to make words with them. I used to get in a right muddle. Jesh would whisper the right words to me and then show me what he'd written so I could see it. Then he'd hide his tablet and make me do it on my own. I got there in the end!

After school was a good time. We'd dawdle home and Jesh would tell me about the flowers and herbs that grew, especially in the springtime. Lovely they was, and he knew their names and what you could use them for. Like cumin is good if you've got something wrong with your eyes or summat, and myrrh makes pain go away. Cinnamon and dill make food taste nice, mustard does too. That's a plant, Jesh said, what has the smallest black seeds and grows so big, birds can nest in it..

When we got home, we had to go and help our dads – Jesh worked in his dad's carpenter shop and I helped my dad in the pottery. Dad would work at his wheel on big pots and bowls, and I'd shape small pots. I was good at that. I made a small pot for me mum and I made one for Jesh's mum Miriam and painted red and black lines round it before dad fired it for me. She said it was the best little pot she had. And Jesh said I'd be a really good potter one day.

But what I remember best was that time when I was ill. I woke up one morning all hot and sticky and aching all over. Mum was a bit worried and went to see Miriam, Jesh's mum.

She brought me a drink with some herbs in it, and Jesh came and sat beside me. He put his hands on my head and it felt nice and cool. He then told me I would get better very soon and talked about how we would go out and play in the fields and help with the harvesting. He told me God was watching over me and all I had to do was believe I would be better. By the evening I was better and we all went to synagogue: dad and me, and Jesh and his dad Joseph.

Jesh told me to say thanks to God for helping me get better. So I did.

I'd do anything for my best friend Jesh.

We was like brothers.

Chapter 3
LITTLE SISTER

Jesus left that place and went back to his home town ... They were all amazed. ... 'Isn't he the carpenter, the son of Mary and brother of James and Joseph and Jude and Simon? Aren't his sisters living here?'
Mark 6: 1, 3; (Matthew 13: 55 - 56)

I wanted to be a boy. Boys have more fun; boys go to school; boys can go out and play around the village. Boys are more important. Everyone knows that. So I said I wanted to be a boy. My poor mother was shocked and told me that girls were just as welcome into the family as boys. She was delighted, she said when her third child was a girl. That was my sister Miriam, named for our mother. I came last, number seven, and mother was just as delighted, or so she said. First in our family was Jesus, then came James, then Miriam. After her, there was Joseph-junior, Simon, Judas, then me. I was named for my mother's sister, Salome, and I think they hoped I would be like her. She is a strong woman, my aunt; keeper of our family history all the way back to King David, and the mother of eight sons. I might have her name but I'm not so lion-hearted, more of a mouse, so Jesus used to say. But mice can be quiet and still in corners, and learn a lot when nobody's looking, he said.

The only time I felt rebellious was when I said I wanted to be a boy. Judas, who's only a year and a bit older than me, had just set off to synagogue school with the others and I wanted to go to school too. I'd listen when after the evening meal the boys would recite what they had learned. Father made sure they had their lessons by heart, and I found I could remember all the words just as well as they did. Better than Simon, who had his head in the clouds and used to forget what he had learnt. But it was when they all had writing tablets and were learning letters and words; I wanted a tablet and to learn to write too. But mother laughed and said there were too many things it was important for a girl to learn, to find time to read and write. So then I said I wished I was a boy. And got told off.

Both Miriam and I worked in the house with mother. She worked hard all the time and we had to work too. We'd help fetch water from the well; at home, we'd gather twigs and stubble for the fire; help grind the grain which mother would form into dough cakes and bake. She also taught us to sew and mend, but I was clumsy with a needle. Miriam was good at sewing so she would do the mending, while I went out and milked the goat, or gathered herbs from the herb patch. Mother would say we both had to learn to do everything a wife needed to do, otherwise we would never find a good husband. But I still didn't see why I couldn't learn to read and write. James used to laugh and tease me.

'So you want to be like one of the famous women in our history? Like Deborah who went into battle with Barak, or Jael, who hammered a tent-peg through Sisera's head?'

'Could they read and write?' I asked.

'I think she'd rather be Queen Esther,' Jesus said, smiling at me.

He never teased me, like James did, but often let me sit beside him in the evening, and watch as he practised letters and words on his wax tablet, telling me what the words meant. He also told me the stories of Deborah and Jael, and Queen Esther. She had saved our people from being completely wiped out and had written a letter wishing all our people peace and directing them to observe the festival of Purim.

'Did she write the letter all by herself?' I wanted to know.

'As far as we know,' Jesus said, 'she was a wise as well as a beautiful woman'.

'All right then,' I said, 'I don't want to be a boy, I want to be like Queen Esther. And learn to read and write.'

Jesus laughed, and said well, why not, he would show me the alphabet and help me write the Shema, which of course I knew. He lent me his tablet and I learned to write:

'Hear O Israel, the Lord our God is one, and you shall love the Lord your God with all your heart and soul and mind and strength.

'Can you write the second part?' Jesus asked. So I carefully added:

'And love your neighbour as yourself'.

I was determined not to forget what I had learnt and would scratch letters in the dust with a stick to practise, and then rub them out with my foot when anyone came by. My father, my brothers and our Rabbi, even mother and Miriam – all disapproved, and said it was not right for a girl to try and be clever and want to learn what the boys learnt – all except Jesus, who told me that every gift came from God and all were of value to him in his kingdom.

'One day,' he said, 'you may find a use for this special gift of yours'.

As things later proved, he was right.

Chapter 4
THE TEMPLE TRADER

Now every year the parents of Jesus went to Jerusalem for the Passover festival. When Jesus was twelve years old, they went to the festival as usual ...

Luke 2: 41 – 42

'He was a bright lad,' I went home and told my wife. 'Up from Galilee for his Bar-Mitzvah I guess. Made an impression on me. Made an impression on the Rabbis too'.

I work at the Court of the Gentiles, a short walk from our house in the Lower City. Each morning early, I'd walk along Small Market Street, exchanging news with friends; grabbing a bread roll fresh from the baker's stall, then through the Bazaar where they sell fruit and fish.

I'm a a money-changer. People come from all over the world to change their foreign money into Temple shekels. Busy place, Court of the Gentiles, especially at festival times. People shouting, arguing, lambs bleating, feet pounding up and down the steps. Noisy. Worse sometimes than the Bazaar! You get used to it.

The boy came and watched me for a while: I was taking in Greek drachmas, Roman denarii, Syrian petas, and giving out shekels for folk to buy sacrifices or make donations to the Temple treasury. It costs a lot to keep this place up and running. I was careful to keep to the rates of exchange, although there were some of us money-changers who would add a peta here or a drachma there and pop this into their own pockets. Everyone knew this went on, turned a blind eye, so to speak. I saw that the boy noticed this with a frown of puzzlement, but his father called to him and he went through the gateway into the Court of the Women. I lost sight of him and his father after that; he probably went on to the Court of the Israelites where the Passover procession was just about to start. Three blasts of the silver trumpet meant the official beginning of Passover sacrifices and we were supposed to stop trading – but there were always latecomers who needed our services, so we carried on with it.

I wondered briefly what the boy was making of it all; I remember my own Bar-Mitzvah, not that long ago, and how puzzling I found it. The priests in their ceremonial robes: all that blue and gold and scarlet – enough to dazzle the eyes. Then the sacrifices, the smell of blood and burning; I had had it all explained to me back then and asked the Passover meal question as instructed, but now, well, I make my own sacrifice and celebrate Passover quietly with my wife without wanting to know all the details of what it means.

I saw the boy several times over the next few days. The Court of the Gentiles is always packed with people from just about everywhere, but somehow, he seemed to stand out from the crowd. Can't say what was special about him though, except his concentration in watching and listening. The Sanhedrin met each day in the Court of the Gentiles to hold public debates on various interpretations of the Law and the Prophets. Not my scene. I have enough trouble remembering the bits of the Law that relate to my own life and work. But this lad was there in the middle, asking question after question. As I said, a Galilean by his accent.

I saw him again, just as I was packing up to go home. He was still talking with some of the scribes, who seemed to be impressed with him. But he must have been here all day! What's more, he was back the next day. And the next.

'You ought to go home, young man,' said one scribe.

'There's so much I need to know,' the boy answered, 'and this place is home'.

Now what did he mean by that? I wondered. Galilee is five days journey from Jerusalem.

Did his parents know he was here? Apparently not, for they arrived a bit later, and in a right old state by the looks of it. They had travelled for a whole day, each of them thinking he was with the other boys.

Then they'd spent days searching the city. He's in for a scolding I thought. He was too, but they weren't too hard on him. Both seemed more puzzled by his behaviour than angry. Perhaps this was the first time he'd done a bunk. Still, he seemed happy to see them and to go back with them.

One thing he did say though, which I thought was strange.

'Didn't you know I would be here? In my Father's house?'

I heard the scribes talking about him when he'd gone.

'Bright lad,' one of them said, ' we'll have to watch out for him when he gets a bit older.'

'I don't know,' said another, slowly. 'He asked too many sharp questions. I have feeling he's going to be trouble. For us all.'

Section 2
THE MINISTRY

Chapter 5
THE PIG FARMER

Then the demons came out of the man and entered the swine, and the herd rushed down the steep bank into the lake, and were drowned.

Luke 8:33

What right did he have to come here and interfere with my pigs? We're not Jews here. Yes, I know they don't like pigs, won't eat pork, say their God told them not to, think they – pigs that is – are dirty creatures. My pigs are not dirty, cleanest, most best-behaved pigs around. Well, they were, till he came along. Even mad old Legion, that's what he called himself, respected my pigs. Used to shout at them from up the hill there, but never did them any harm.

Poor old Legion. He'd come and talk to me in his quieter times. But mad as moon-dogs could make him he was. His talk never made much sense. Used to say he was full of them, said they tormented him, pricked him all over with pins and needles. Made him tear off his clothes and cut himself with stones. They shouted things inside his head, he said. Worse still, when he was trying to sleep, they whispered wicked things at him. I wanted to know what sort of wicked things, but he laughed madly and said,

'You don't want to know, mate.' Then he ran off.

The folk in the village tried to get him to stay in his house, but he wouldn't. Couldn't breathe in the house he told me. They tried to chain him up. Bound both his hands and his feet with chains, but he tore them off too. Lived mostly in the burial caves and went shouting and hollering up in the hills. Could hear him for miles when the fits were on him. But he never harmed anyone, as far as I knew. Only himself.

But then – he came. The prophet. Chap that was going round preaching to the Jews and healing people, they said. Why did he come here? Like I said, we're not Jews. Well, maybe there are plenty who could do with a bit of healing, but we don't want him preaching at us. Still, give him his due, he didn't. What he did was … well it was unbelievable. If I hadn't been around and seen it happen, I wouldn't have believed it.

They'd come across the lake and as soon as the boat was beached, old Legion came running and shouting down from among the tombs. Fell flat on his face when he got to the prophet and shouted,

'Get out of here! Mind your own business. We know who you are, you're the son of High God! Get out and leave us alone!'

By then he was sobbing,

'Don't torture us!'

The prophet just stood and said quite quietly,

'Come out of this man, leave him alone'.

Then he asked,

'What's your name?'

The poor chap managed to gasp out,

'Legion. I'm Legion. There are lots of us. Don't send us back to the hell we came from.'

It was the sudden hush that alerted me. I'm used to all my pigs snuffling and snorting and rootling around, but they'd all gone quiet. Several were lying down, none of them were feeding. It was like they'd suddenly all got the swine disease that makes them go miserable, then mad.

I went to pick up a couple of piglets, when suddenly they all began to move. Headed out to the cliff. Began to run and shove each other, pushing and trampling, squealing and grunting, running as though all the demons of Legion were after them. Or … in them. I began to run and shouted to my mates to come and help me herd them back, but no-one moved. Nothing moved. Except all my pigs. Straight over the cliff they went and I heard the splash, splash, splash as they hit the water of the lake below. The water swirled and eddied madly. Then grew still. Everything went still. My mates had all legged it back to the village. Some mates!

I stood and looked across at the prophet and his men. They all looked shocked. The prophet came across to me, put his hand on my shoulder and said quietly:

'I'm sorry. It had to be like this. The man Legion needed to know, and to know for certain his demons had been sent out of him, and would not return. Your pigs were the means of showing him that as they are now drowned and gone for ever, so are the devils that have haunted him all his life.

Can you accept that?'

I did not know what to say, so said nothing. Then he said:

'Come and see Legion now. Although I think he will need a new name.'

'His name's Romanus', I croaked. 'I knew his family. His father was a Roman soldier.'

'Then meet the new Romanus', the prophet said.

Chapter 6
A HUNGRY BOY

Jesus looked round and saw a large crowd coming towards him, so he asked Philip: 'Where can we go to buy enough food for all these people?'
Andrew. said: 'There is a boy here who has five loaves of barley bread and two fish. But they will certainly not be enough for all these people?'
John 6: 5, 8 (Matthew 14: 15 – 20; Luke 9: 10 – 17)

I'd seen the boy. Skipping ahead like a young lamb, or a leaping fish. Had he slipped out and headed for the hills instead of going demurely to synagogue school? Would he find it was worth it, this freedom? Worth what he would have to face from an irate Rabbi and a disappointed grandmother? Obviously, in his eyes. Have fun now and face the consequences later!

That spirit of rebellion, that quirk of nature which won't face up to likely difficulties and lives in hope that one would not be found out, I know it well. I had it, back in the days of my own springtime, when I too would slip away after household duties were done. Slip out of my parent's clutches. They were busy arranging a suitable match for me, to a much older man, and one not at all to my liking. So, like the wayward lamb I was, I ran away. And paid the price.

So now I have returned to my home town. Older, almost unrecognisable I found, which suited me. Wiser? Regretting the hurt I caused my elderly parents? Maybe, maybe.

But the boy. I knew him, although he was of course older, much taller, with gangly limbs. He had always been hungry I remembered. His parents were both dead, so he lived with his grand-mother, whom I also knew. She had been kind to me in my younger days.

I kept the boy in sight as we found ourselves joining a group of people climbing a hill, all heading in one direction. Where were they – where were we – all going? What impulse was carrying us all, now quite a crowd, in the same direction?

'The prophet,' was whispered about me. 'The story teller. The miracle worker. The healer. He's here'.

'What? Who?'

'Jesus-bar-Joseph. That's who'.

I had heard of him, and his teaching, outcast as I

was, but I'd never taken much notice. I had been keeping my head down, as I did now. I'd also heard of his healing powers. Could be heal the hurt in my soul?

We reached the place. The boy. Me. And what seemed to be several hundred others. We listened to his stories: tales of a lost sheep, a wayward son. Well, I could relate to those. But to find a father's forgiveness? Of that I was not so sure. But the words of the prophet continued to ring in my memory:

'Don't be afraid. Don't trust in your own wealth. Don't argue. Don't worry about things. Look at the birds, at the flowers. See their beauty. Trust in God. There is forgiveness for all'.

I turned to go away, when I heard one of the prophet's men saying the people must be getting tired and hungry. He asked how they could be fed in this lonely place. What would it take to provide food for all these people? But, I thought, wouldn't people have brought food for themselves? I had brought nothing, but then I had nothing and was used to hunger; surely other folk couldn't all have been on the edge of starvation, like me. Most of them would have set out with a few bits of bread, a morsel of goat cheese, a few small fish. Why didn't they take it out for themselves? Suddenly

I knew the answer – they didn't want to share, even with those who had nothing; they might not have had enough!

I looked for the boy. Always hungry, he would have been given a bite of lunch by his kindly grandmother. He had been near enough to hear the talk about feeding the people and he now went up to the prophet's man, and to my complete astonishment … offered his own lunch!

The man didn't laugh, although he might have done. He took the five small buns and a couple of sardines with a smile of amusement, probably thinking, what indeed is that for so many?

But he took the gift and gave it to the prophet Jesus. A hungry boy's small bit of food. All he had. The prophet took them and blessed them, broke the tiny loaves and told his men to share them with – everybody!

There was a sense of relaxation, and laughter. People pulled out their own food and began to share with others. A woman offered me some bread. One of the men came with a piece of goat's cheese. We talked about the stories we had heard. I saw the boy, helping the men gather up the crumbs. Not only had there been enough for everyone, but there was some left over!

It was a miracle of sharing, of giving, of unstinting generosity and kindliness.

And it all began with a hungry boy.

Would I have had the courage to do the same?

Chapter 7
ONE OF SEVENTY-TWO

... the Lord chose another seventy-two and sent them out two by two... He said to them ... don't take a purse, a beggar's bag, or shoes ...
Luke 10: 1, 4

That was the day! Jesus came and said he had a job for me, well, not only me, there were seventy-two of us. He was sending us out to towns and villages round about to tell people good news and heal any who were sick. Our task was to tell his stories, talk about his healing and where necessary, to carry out such healing ourselves. Well, that was the plan. Right, I thought and rushed to get my travel bag. I'd need spare sandals, a spare shirt, a skin of water, a bit of food, maybe some money ...

But then Jesus came and took the bag away!

'You won't need any of that', he said. 'I want you to go with nothing'.

'Nothing?'

'You can take a walking stick. Otherwise, go as you are', he said.

'But Jesus,' I began to protest, only to find he had slipped away. A habit he had when we started to argue.

I don't mind telling you I was a bit miffed by this. Go as you are indeed! How were we supposed to manage that? He'd said we were to stay where we were made welcome. But what if we weren't welcomed? Well then apparently, we were to simply walk away. That was all very well, I thought, but I could imagine getting rather tired, and rather hungry and having nowhere to go, and nowhere to stay.

But then I remembered I had made a promise to follow him. Hadn't I? And that meant doing as I was told. And I did trust him. Didn't I?

So I went. Very nervous. Most of us were. Could we do this? Could I do this? But he said we were to go in pairs, two together, to help each other along a bit. I went with Melchi, good chap. Had a good loud voice for one thing and never let anyone or anything bother him.

We went to the first village; Melchi went to the market place, and I went to the well where the women were gathered.

'Hey, people! I come with stories of good news for you!'

They listened as I told them about Jesus: what he did to heal sick folk; his stories; his teaching. They asked if he could come and help a girl who couldn't walk properly, and I said Jesus had told me to try to heal her. I asked her name, and then I took her hand and said:

'Hannah, in Jesus' name, you can walk'.

I helped her up, she was a bit frightened and clung to my hand, but after a few wobbles, she stood straight and still. I held tight to her hand as she began, slowly at first to take a few steps. Then … I let go. That was an amazing feeling, a joy and a wonder to see her look of astonishment as she literally found her feet.

As evening drew in Hannah's grandmother invited me to supper at her house, and then said I could spend the night. She would find me anything I needed. So that was a lovely welcome and I left next day after wishing her and her family peace. Melchi did all right for himself, got bedded down with the innkeeper.

Could this happen again? We went on the the next place, a bit busier, more people, all very intent on their own business. This time I went to the market place, and feeling very uncertain began with the same words:

'Hey, people, I come with stories of good news for you'.

It wasn't so easy this time. A few people stopped, many simply went on their way, some laughed and shook their heads. But I went on to tell the few who were there some of the stories Jesus told: the ones about a lost coin, a lost sheep, and the wilful son who went off and spent all his legacy. When dusk came, a man came up to me and said would I come and have supper with him and his wife, who, he said, made wonderful bread. He wanted his wife to hear the story of the young lad who had gone off with his father's money and spent it all. They had, he said, a son who had stolen money from them and run away, and they were feeling bitter and angry.

'He is no longer my son,' the man said. 'He has no place here'.

I reminded them that in Jesus' story, the son had been welcomed home when he came back with his tail between his legs. They were very thoughtful after that. But they gave me a bed for the night, and next day, before I left I wished them peace, and the hope their son would return, and that they might find it in their hearts to forgive him.

Both Melchi and I travelled round a bit more after that; talking about Jesus and his message, and to my astonishment, healing people. Everywhere, people came with offers of hospitality: food and water, and somewhere to stay. Sometimes we both got a billet in the same place, other times we went to separate houses. In the poorer places, the rooms were a bit rough and ready, but who minds that? The whole experience was scary ... but wonderful.

Jesus himself said that: trust in God, he said, and you will find that doing God's work is scary, but also wonderful.

Chapter 8
HEALING AT THE POOL

Near the Sheep Gate in Jerusalem there is a pool with five porches. In Hebrew it is called Bethzatha. A large crowd of sick people were lying in the porches – the blind, the lame and the paralysed.
John 5: 2 – 3

I've wondered what I did wrong, what sin I committed, to have a boy born a cripple. Not that we knew that when he was born. He was a very small baby, and quiet. All my friends commented on how lucky I was to have such a quiet baby, who cried so little and didn't wriggle and worm his way out of his swaddling bands.

But then, when it was time for him to sit, to stand, to walk, he couldn't do any of that. He flopped. His legs were thin and wasted. All the other babies in our circle of motherhood were busy exploring their worlds, getting under their mothers' feet, getting into mischief. My friends' comments changed then; instead of being told I was a lucky woman, there were looks of pity, and murmurs of blame, thinly disguised as commiseration.

What would his life be like? What could he do other than become a beggar? Just lie here all day, shaking his begging cup at passers-by? He is now twelve years old, and we should be planning the joyful celebration of his Bar-Mitzvah. But the Rabbi merely shook his head when my husband mentioned the possibility. So each day his father brings him here to the Pool of Bethzatha, and when my work is done, I come and sit with him. We sit together, waiting for the angel to come and stir the water. When that happens, the first one to touch the moving water will be healed. But that has only happened twice in all the years we have been here, and each time, someone else has touched the water before we can get anywhere near. As the water begins to stir and ripple, people crowd round, pushing each other out of the way sometimes. Mattathias simply laughs and tells me not to worry, not to push him.

'I might fall in', he tells me. 'That water is very deep, they say, and unless you could hold me up, I'd sink to the bottom. If there is a bottom that is, many people say it goes down for ever!'

He's such a bright and cheerful boy, observant too. We sit and talk, and he tells me many things about the other folk here.

'See that man over there?' he said. 'He's blind now, but he used to be a scribe and a teacher, writing out interpretations of the Law and stories of the Prophets for the boys in school. He's got it all in his head, so he doesn't need to see, he says. We sit together sometimes and he's taught me the Ten Commandments, the Laws of Moses, and some of the teachings of the Prophets. Just because I'm here, doesn't mean I can't learn a little. I think he misses teaching, so is glad to have me try and learn from him.'

I was surprised; such a thing had not occurred to me; he had not been able to go to school, so how could he learn?

'There's a girl over there,' he went on, 'she can walk but not very well, but what's worse for her is she can't use her hands. They are twisted and her fingers are curled up. And when I watch you at home, mother, with all the things you do: making bread, cooking, spinning, weaving, mending, well, I think: what's going to happen to her?'

What indeed? I thought. And what's going to happen to you? And why are you talking about all these other people? What good is that going to do?

The water began to bubble. We all knew the signs. There's a faint rumbling that seems to come up from the depths of the water and ripples appear across the surface. Those of us who are helpers get up and prepare to move our poor ones to be the first to touch the water; to grab the opportunity of being healed. Mattathias puts his hand on my arm and pulls me back.

'Let the others go,' he said. 'I am well enough.'

I looked at him in utter astonishment; did he not want to get well? I wanted to help him push and shove our way forward as well as the others. But Mattathias held on to my hand.

'I am well enough,' he repeated.

It was the girl who got to the water; her helper – a young man, probably her brother, who looked big and strong enough to push through any crowd, got her there and held her hands under the now fast rippling water. She was laughing and crying at the same time.

'So cold', we heard her say, ' the water is so cold.'

The water bubbled, then grew quiet and still. She took her hands out and held them out to her brother who dried them gently. I could see she was moving her fingers, straightening them and bending them as though testing their ability to move. The young man led her away.

'I am glad it was her,' said my son quietly. I hope she can live well. It would also be good if the man over there could get to the water, but there is no-one to help him. His family don't want to know him, he says, and he has no friends. Says its his own fault. He has been here many years.'

'So might you be, my son,' I said, unable to hide the disappointment of having missed this opportunity. What could I tell my husband, who would be both upset and angry that we had not tried hard enough to get our son well. He had so wanted a son who could take over the family business, not a helpless cripple. He would blame me for not trying hard enough. Mattathias read my thoughts.

'Not your fault, mother,' he said. 'We could not have reached the water in time. No need to reproach yourself. My time will come and in the meantime, others' needs are greater than mine.'

The next few days were busy for me. I had the Passover Festival feast to prepare for, which involved much baking. Mattathias spent the time alone by the Pool. When I went with my husband to fetch him later, he was bursting with excitement.

'Do you remember the cripple man I told you about? The one who had been at the Pool for many years?

Well' … he paused dramatically … 'he is cured!'

'Who helped him into the water?' I wanted to know.

'No-one! It was the healer, Jesus-bar-Joseph who came and asked him if he wanted to get well. Then told him to pick up his mat … and walk!'

I very nearly told him not to be so silly. He must have been dreaming, or something. But my husband Nahum said it was true. He had seen it all when he went to fetch Mattathias. The man had struggled to his feet, Jesus holding him firmly by the hand, and taken a few uncertain steps. Then a few more, and a few more, a huge smile on his face. Then he picked up his mat and walked slowly but steadily away. Mattathias was laughing.

'It was so wonderful to see,' he said.

Why not you? I thought. Why not heal you my son? Why could you not have asked this Jesus-bar-Joseph to heal you? Where is he? Can't we find him? So many questions went round my head, I almost missed what Mattathias was saying.

'He, Jesus, asked the man if he wanted to get well'.

'Stupid question,' I said angrily, 'of course he would want to get well. Wouldn't he?'

'Maybe. But then, maybe not. He asked me too.'

'What?'

'He asked if I wanted to be well. I said I would like to be well, but if I were not here, the blind scribe would not have a pupil. The girl and the crippled man would not have had someone to talk to. I can be of use here'.

Words failed me. I could not understand this at all. My husband lifted our son ready to carry him home. Mattathias smiled at me.

'Don't worry mother, I am well enough,' he said.

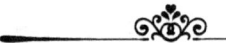

Section 3
TOWARDS JERUSALEM

Chapter 9
PHILIP AND THE DONKEY

As Jesus and his disciples approached Jerusalem they came to Bethphage at the Mount of Olives. There, Jesus sent two of the disciples on ahead, with these instructions: Go to the village there ahead of you and at once you will find a donkey tied up, with her colt beside her. Untie them and bring them to me'.
Matthew 21: 1 – 2; (Mark 11: 1 – 11; Luke 19: 28 – 40; John 12: 12 - 29)

Philip was eight years old, one of five children. He lived in Galilee, although he was not Jewish, he was Greek. There were many Greeks in Galilee at that time; it was a good place to live. Philip's older brothers worked on the farm with their father; they were all tall and strong; his sister helped their mother at home. She was two years younger than Philip but already taller and stronger than he was. Philip had been very ill when he was two years old, and was now small and crippled. His legs were too thin to support him and had little strength in them; he couldn't walk properly and herpled round the village on the two crutches his father had made for him. Whenever the family had to travel any distance, either

Philip stayed at home with his aunt, or else he rode on the donkey. His father had also made a special saddle for him, with a high back to support him and straps to hold him in. He hated it.

His name in Greek means 'lover of horses' and he loved horses. He dreamed of one day riding a big horse, perhaps a big black, or a grey. He'd seen the horses the Roman officers rode and he dreamed of being big and strong and riding into a city like Jerusalem, looking down on people from the back of a great horse. So he hated the small patient donkey which carried him, and indeed carried many other things: bundles of hay, or sticks; water carriers; panniers of fruit and vegetables, all without complaining. What the donkey thought of Philip, we shall never know, but they are gentle creatures, and very forgiving.

Although Philip and his family were Greek, he went to the local synagogue school, where he heard the stories of the Jewish prophets and learnt too of the One God the Jews believed in. But he also learnt about the Roman and Greek world from his parent, their heroes and emperors, and he added these to his dreams.

One day he heard in synagogue school the prophecy of Zechariah, about a king, triumphant and victorious, but riding on a donkey! Philip thought that was utter nonsense, kings rode horses didn't they? But he was not allowed to say that to the Rabbi.

Philip also heard stories about a new prophet, called Jesus-bar-Joseph; who came from Nazareth, near Philip's home, and who healed sick people, told amazing stories and taught new and wonderful things. He was, some people said, the great Messiah-King.

'He'll never ride a donkey,' thought Philip to himself, 'he'll have the biggest horse!'

And he imagined Jesus, the Messiah-King, in gorgeous robes riding a wonderful horse with a silvery coat and with the saddle and bridle shining with bright, beautiful colours.

One Passover time, Philip's family went with Jewish friends and neighbours up to Jerusalem for the festival. Philip had to ride that hated donkey in that hated saddle while everyone else walked. It was a happy occasion; people sang, told stories and jokes and there was a lot of fun and laughter. As they came near the city, the excitement increased as news came back that they were going to join the prophet Jesus-bar-Joseph who was riding up ahead.

Philip bounced in his saddle and craned to see the big horse Jesus must be riding, but as they came nearer, all he could see was – a man on a donkey! An ordinary man, on an ordinary little grey donkey!

'That's him!' people were shouting, 'that's Jesus of Nazareth! Hosanna! Blessed is he who comes in the name of the Lord!'

They waved palm branches and sang, and spread their cloaks on the ground in front of him.

Philip felt sick with disappointment, this couldn't be right! But his own wise little donkey knew better, it trotted faster and faster, pushing and nudging a way through the crowd till it was right behind the one Jesus was riding. And Jesus turned and looked at Philip, and smiled at him with such kindliness and understanding that nearly made Philip cry. But he was a Greek boy of eight and he didn't cry. He knew that, although this man was riding a donkey – just like his – somehow, he rode like a king. So Philip sat up straighter, and rode proudly into Jerusalem, behind the king.

All that week, Philip's father came back from the market place with tales of what Jesus had been doing: telling stories; healing the blind and crippled. Philip bounced in his chair.

'Would he heal me?' he asked.

His father was doubtful.

'We could ask,' he said, 'but you've been a cripple since you were small. No harm in asking though.'

It was the most amazing miracle, Philip later told everyone. He and his father went to the Temple, to the Court of the Gentiles, Philip swinging along on his crutches, where they met Jesus.

'I rode behind you,' Philip said to the healer, 'cos I thought you would be riding a great big horse, but you had a little donkey, just like mine. So I wanted to be just like you. Please can you help me walk, so I can follow you?'

Jesus laughed.

'Do you really believe I can heal you?' he asked.

Philip could only nod, speechlessly. Jesus stretched out his hand and touched him. 'Be well,' he said.

Philip and his family were still in Jerusalem the following Friday, and they could not believe it when Jesus, the prophet, the king Philip had followed into the city, the healer who had made him well, was condemned as a criminal and led out to die a dreadful death. On a cross.

And this time, Greek boy of eight or not, Philip cried bitterly.

Chapter 10
THE NEW CLOAK

Many people spread their cloaks on the road, while others cut branches in the fields and spread them on the road.
Mark 11: 8

Jonas was a potter in Nazareth of Galilee. He made good pots, but he didn't make a good living, because he would sell his pots cheaply to any poor widow who came with but two small copper coins in her purse.

'Too kind-hearted for his own good,' his wife Joanna would grumble.

She was a thrifty soul who scrimped and saved, patched and mended and kept herself and her husband clean and neat. Especially when it came to Jonas' old cloak, his only cloak. It had been a good cloak which did double duty: it kept him warm and dry when he went out to work on cold days, and it covered them both as they slept at night. But it was very old and had been patched carefully with old cloth, no use using new cloth as any good housewife would tell you. In fact it had been patched so many times that you could scarcely see the original material.

But one day, not long before Passover, Jonas sold a large batch of pots to a Roman centurion, who recognised quality when he saw it and gave a good price for them. Delighted, both Jonas and Joanna agreed he would have a new cloak.

That year, as every year in the spring month of Nissan, they went up to Jerusalem for the Passover festival and Joanna carefully packed the new cloak for use when they got to the city, taking the old one to use on the journey. They joined the usual crowd of pilgrims: friends travelling together, sharing memories of previous trips, telling stories, asking after relatives no longer able to travel with them, and remembering those who had died. Sooner or later, Joanna thought, they'll start talking about Jesus-bar-Joseph, the prophet who was making something of a name for himself. Living as they did in the small town of Nazareth, where Jesus had grown up, she and Jonas knew his family well and were as puzzled as anyone over this eldest son, who had left home and gone travelling round the country. Greatly to the annoyance of his brothers who were left to run the carpentry business and support the rest of the family.

Strange tales came back to them: of his teaching, of his healing: how he could restore sight and hearing, make a lame man walk again, cure leprosy, even cast out demons. Jonas was completely bowled over by these tales, and became more and more convinced that their Jesus was special – really special – perhaps even, the Messiah! Joanna was more sceptical and reserved judgement. She wasn't at all sure what to think.

As they came nearer to Jerusalem, Jonas went on ahead. He wanted to make sure they found a good place to stay. Joanna walked with the other women. After a while, they became aware of a bit of a commotion up ahead: shouting, singing, an air of excitement. Jonas came running back.

'Quick! The cloak, where's the cloak? It's our Jesus up ahead, riding a donkey like in the prophecy, and they're putting cloaks down for him to ride on!'

Before Joanna could stop him, he'd riffled through the bags and pulled out the new cloak, and run off with it.

'Hey!' his wife shouted, 'take the old one!'

But he didn't hear. She scurried after him clutching the old cloak and caught up with him, just as … she couldn't believe what she was seeing! The silly man was putting the beautiful new cloak on the ground for the donkey to walk on!

'It'll be ruined!' she cried out, 'donkey's hooves all over it, and suppose the animal does something on it. Oh, I can't bear it!'

Everyone around her was waving branches and shouting 'Hosanna!' and 'Blessed is he!' but poor Joanna was hardly aware of it all. Hardly even aware of the man on the donkey, until he turned and looked at her, with kindly sympathy, as though he understood all her anxieties. She let the crowd go by, and sat down by the roadside, and wept.

Jonas came back and found her. He was carrying the new cloak.

'My poor wife,' he said, 'I know what you're worrying about. But look,' and he shook out the cloak, 'not a mark on it. Not even the tiniest tear. Now, tell me, isn't that a miracle?'

He wrapped the cloak round her, for she was shivering.

'Just think Joanna. That was the Messiah-King who rode by – on our cloak. How could we have given him anything less than our very best?'

Later that week in Jerusalem, Jonas and Joanna heard another commotion, about a particular criminal, who was going to be crucified.

'Its that so-called prophet,' everyone was saying, 'the one who was supposed to be a healer. Said to have spouted a lot of blasphemies. Name of Jesus-bar-Joseph.'

'It can't be, it can't be,' poor Jonas cried. 'What did he do? He went about doing good. He healed a lot of people, he never did anything wrong. It can't be all over!'

That night they huddled under the new cloak and wept together in despair.

Jonas and Joanna stayed in Jerusalem for a few more days trying to understand what had happened, and why. But then strange news came to them. It was not all over.

There was more to come.

Chapter 11
THE BOY WHO SHOUTED TO STONES

….the large crowd of his disciples began to thank God and praise him in loud voices … saying:
'God bless the King who comes in the name of the Lord' …
Some of the Pharisees in the crowd spoke to Jesus: 'Teacher, order your disciples to be quiet'. Jesus answered: 'I tell you that if they keep quiet, the very stones would cry out'.
Luke 19: 37, 39 – 40

Eliel was ten years old, but to look at him you would have guessed his age to be about six, maybe seven. Like many children at that time, he was small for his age, and a bright, cheerful child. But he was blind. He knew his world by touch: the roughness of the donkey's coat; the hardness of the stones, his mother's smooth face. He also listened. Each day his father brought him to the city gate and from this position he could hear the noises of the city, footsteps, donkeys trotting, the creak of wagons and carts and people's voices. There was a constant stream of people coming in from the villages to bring goods to the markets, returning home in the evening. He would listen to the different sounds their footsteps made, sounding hollow as they came into the porch of the gate, echoing under the arches.

Every day he listened to people going in and out of the city. He recognised the voices of many of them as they passed him each day and would call out a greeting,

'Blessings on you,' as he shook his begging bowl.

Occasionally a woman might stop and talk with him for a few minutes, but usually, they passed on their way. Some folk might drop a coin in his bowl, but many people never noticed him at all. He could have been invisible. All day he sat by the city gate, until his father came to take him home in the evening.

On a day which he would always remember as the most important day of his life, he heard a procession pass through the gate. At first, he did not think of it as anything special; he just noticed there were suddenly more people than usual, coming down from the Mount of Olives. There were running footsteps, shouting, and the soft swish of palm branches waving. From his position on the ground, Elial was very aware of the pattering of many feet and a swirl of air, as people threw down cloaks. Then came the clip-clop of a donkey's hooves, and a lot of cheering and shouting,

'Hosanna! Hosanna to the son of David! Blessed is he who comes in the name of the Lord!'

Elial wanted to know who was this son of David, but no-one was able to stop and tell him.

The procession stopped for a while by the gate, and Elial heard some other people, Pharisees by the sound of them, muttering crossly and telling the man to order his followers to stop shouting and be quiet. But the man said that even if they stopped, the very stones would cry out.

All went quiet as the crowd passed on into the city. The boy was alone. Suddenly he shouted out 'Hosanna!' as loud as he could and to his surprise, the stones did echo back to him: '...sanna'. All that rest of that day into the evening, when he thought he was alone, he would shout out 'Hosanna!' and listen for the stones of the gate to cry out: '...sanna, '...sanna!

When evening came, he heard the man's voice as he and his followers came back, leading the donkey this time. Elias suddenly shouted: 'Hosanna!' and the man stopped and came to him.

'Hello', he said, 'what are you shouting?'

'I'm making the stones cry out,' Elias explained, 'They do, because you said they would. They have cried out to me all day. I have to sit here because I cannot see you and I couldn't follow you into the city, so I shouted to the stones'.

The man squatted down beside him.

'Would you like to be able to follow me?' he asked.

What a question! Elias could hardly whisper 'Yes' because he suddenly wanted that so much. He felt the man gently touch his face, and felt a wetness on his eyes. He blinked several times, and found the dim light he had always been able to see become slowly brighter. There were shapes in the brightness, shadows and outlines, movements that linked with the sounds he knew so well. The donkey stirred and shuffled his feet, and Elias suddenly knew what the donkey looked like. He turned his head and heard the man's voice:

'It will take a little while to get used to your new world'.

Elias watched the man's face as he said this, and found he could recognise what a kindly smile looked like. His own face reflected his wonder and delight.

'Live well,' the man said.

The man, his friends and the donkey all disappeared towards Bethany, and Elias watched with joy and astonishment the colours of the sun as it went down behind the hills, and the violet shadows come creeping up. At first he was anxious about the shadows, but was reassured when he heard footsteps and the familiar voice of his father. He looked wonderingly at him as he told his story, taking in every feature of the father whose voice he knew so well. His father knew at once who the man was.

'That was Jesus, the teacher and healer. And he healed you – you who've been blind from birth! I never thought such a thing would be possible!'

'I am going to follow him,' Elias declared.

So he did. Followed Jesus all through the week, watching as he taught and healed in the market place and in the Temple courtyard; followed Jesus through the events of that dreadful Friday, at which Elias raged, and could not understand. Then on into the amazing events of the third miraculous day.

All his life, Elias told his story, never forgetting how he had once sat by the Temple Gate of Jerusalem and made the very stones cry out 'Hosanna!'

Chapter 12
THE PERFUME SELLER

Mary took half a litre of very expensive perfume made of pure nard, poured it on Jesus' feet and wiped them with her hair.
John 12: 3 (Matthew 26 7; Mark 14: 3)

There is a skill to making perfume, an art and a skill. I have that skill and have been making and selling perfume for more than twenty years now. My name is Julia, a Roman name you will note. My father was a Roman soldier, who came to Jerusalem with the army and remained when he received his army pension, to marry a Jewish girl, my mother. Thus I was brought up, like many others we knew, with a foot in both cultures, so to speak.

In his travels with the Roman army my father had marched the spice roads, and became interested in the herbs and spices traded from far away places. So with his pension he opened our shop, selling ointments, medicines and of course, perfume. It prospered, people flocked to buy frankincense, hyssop, aloes, wormwood, gall, myrrh, saffron, galbanum. We stocked them all, and of course, the most favoured and costly of all – spikenard.

My mother taught me from a young age how to turn these expensive ingredients into the best perfumes. I learned to make sweet ointments for a lady's hands by spreading layers of petals on the lanolin of sheep's wool, or pounding them with mutton fat; I could drop seeds, crushed roots and flowers into hot olive oil and later strain it to make a simple scent. But the best way was to take the root, leaves and flowers of spikenard, put them into a bag, press and turn and squeeze them to extract the natural oils. Handfuls of flowers and leaves to make but a few drops of scented oil. This was then stored in small, fine alabaster jars.

As I grew older I was allowed to serve in the shop. Who came to buy? Well of course the army wives and daughters from the garrison; maidservants buying for the rich ladies of Herod's court; men sometimes, buying a gift for wife or sweetheart. And then, always late in the evening, came the ladies of the night. They always had good money to spend.

At first, my mother was reluctant to let me serve these women, who came with their henna-painted nails and darkened eyelashes, who wore their hair loose on their shoulders. They were always well-dressed and would come into the shop in twos and threes, laughing together. But behind the bright smiles, their eyes were sad, a little wary, sometimes fearful.

But one I remember in particular, although it has been many years since she came. It was late one evening, like the night women, but alone. She wore no make-up, had no jewellery, and her hair was modestly bound under her head-dress. She also seemed poorly dressed compared to others whom I had served.

But she had money, plenty of it. She bought one of our alabaster jars of spikenard and carried it away carefully into the night. I turned to my mother, puzzled.

'Who was she?' I wanted to know. 'Do you know her?'

For my mother had nodded to her as to an acquaintance.

Yes, she knew her. Her name was Mary, from Bethany. She lives quietly with her brother Lazarus and older sister Martha, mother said. But it was not always so. Mary was the wild one, the one who wanted adventure, who stole off into the night and went to the garrison towns of Caesarea and Sepphoris, who earned a good living – if it can be called 'good' – among the soldiers of the towns. I thought of the women I had served with their sad eyes. Was it really good living?

'No', said my mother firmly. 'Money yes, in plenty sometimes. But good? No.'

Mary became seriously ill, worn and frightened. She called it her demon time, and would not have survived it if she had not met a wandering preacher and healer. Light dawned on me.

'You mean Jesus-bar-Joseph? From Nazareth? The miracle worker?'

We had heard of him, and the stories of his healing powers, making the blind see, the deaf hear and speak, the lame to walk. And causing a storm among the religious leaders of our day.

Then of course there was Lazarus! I hadn't remembered the name earlier, but of course, Lazarus! Brought back from the dead by this Jesus, they said. Something that even now I find hard to believe. So Mary was Lazarus' sister! And she had been a pr- ... my mother stopped my mouth.

'Don't speak of it!' she said.

But why did she want the perfume? I thought, but did not say. And how was it she had all that money? My mother told me the family were not rich; they had no servants and Martha did the work of the house. Had Mary earned it from a satisfied client? And kept it? But I knew better than to ask mother! Later, much later, I learned the rest of the story.

Jesus came as a guest to their house. Martha, the practical one, was busy with preparing the meal. Lazarus had come in from his work and Mary came, with her jar of the most expensive perfume there is, and poured it over Jesus' feet! And she had loosened her long hair, remembering her former life, and wiped his feet with it. Of course there was an outcry!

I think back to the time when she came to us and I had wanted to know, who was this woman? I know now. She was one who wanted to turn her life around, who needed forgiveness, acceptance, recognition and healing, and found it at Jesus' feet. She had listened to his stories, sought understanding of his teaching, marvelled at his kindness to her, to her sister and most of all to her brother. She was one who poured out her love in an act of extravagant contrition at a time when Jesus needed it most.

I remain grateful that I was the one who had made the perfume she bought, a symbol of her former life; I had sold it to her and had thus played a minor role in her salvation.

Chapter 13
THE TEMPLE TRADER - AGAIN

> *Jesus went into the Temple and drove out all those who were buying and selling there. He overturned the tables of the money-changers, and the stools of those who sold pigeons ...*
> *Matthew 21: 12 (Mark 11: 15; Luke 19: 45 – 48; John 2: 13 - 22)*

I've been at this job for nearly forty years. How much coinage has passed through my hands in that time ? Greek, Roman, Egyptian, Syrian, Phrygian, I've handled them all and changed them into shekels for the Temple tax. Many traders charge a fee for changing money, the qolbon, or quarter-shekel, with another quarter if the coin given exceeds the tax, and this would often slip into the traders' own purse. Many a time I've seen it happen. Sometimes visitors would give a donation to the Temple treasury, which was supposed to go towards the upkeep of the Temple, but again this would disappear. But my father brought me up to respect the Law, and all people. He was in this job fifty years and never once, as far as I know, overcharged. Neither do I.

I've seen all kinds of folk come and go, visiting the Temple, some for the first time when lads come up for their

Bar-Mitzvah ceremonies, with proud fathers and mothers and shy sisters; visitors from all over the world; bringing in their animals for sacrifices, which were always rejected as unsuitable so that only those sold here would be accepted. And of course, cost twice as much. I've seen all kinds of scamp traders come and go: those who had no more respect for the Law and the Prophets than the doves and lambs and calves they sold at vastly inflated prices. Probably less.

I've witnessed all kinds of strange events in and around the Temple precincts. One particular day stands out, although it began like any other. It was the day the prophet came, the one they called Jesus-bar-Joseph, the one who met a sticky end later that week. I'd heard of him, who hadn't? He'd made a name for himself around the country with all kinds of miracles of healing and unorthodox teaching. Upset the authorities more than somewhat and got himself a price on his head so they say.

Well, I didn't think he would have the pluck to show his face here in Jerusalem, but wouldn't you know it? He turned up here, not only in the city, but actually here in the Temple! Came in and looked all around, and didn't look too impressed either. Most folk come in and gasp and gawk and say how great it all is. Which it is in some ways.

Next day, he was back. Looking determined. But what came next I wouldn't have believed if I hadn't seen it with my own eyes. He marched past my small table near the entrance and went straight to old Esli's table … and turned it over! Piles of coins rolled everywhere and Esli went screaming and scrabbling after them. He then went on to other tables and did the same; he drove out the lambs and calves penned up for the sacrifices, knocked over the barriers and with a shove on their behinds sent the animals all stumbling and pushing their way out into the street; he flung open the cages of the doves, who all went fluttering up and out as fast as wings could take them. What a to-do! Shouts and curses; sheep bleating, cattle mooing, feet clattering as stall holders tried to grab their goods. And over it all his voice: a great voice like thunder,

'This is my Father's House, not a market place! A place for prayer, not a place for thieves!'

He strode out. The place looked like a war zone. Esli, Habib and the others were still grabbing what coins they could find, and the animal traders were out in the street trying to round up their sheep and cattle. I went to lend a hand, and it was only then I realised something. Jesus-bar-Joseph had passed me by. My table, with its stacks of small coins was just as it had been. Had I imagined it or had he paused by my table, and put his hand briefly on my shoulder? And his words: 'my Father's house' – where had I heard them before?

It was much later, telling the story to my wife, that it came back to me.

It was the boy, all those years ago, who had said:

'Didn't you know I would be in my Father's House?'

Chapter 14
THE TALE OF A SOLDIER

When they came to the place that is called The Skull, they crucified Jesus there ...'
Luke 23: 33 (Matthew 27: 35; Mark 15: 24; John 19: 18)

I'm retired now, thank all the gods. Or thank the one God, whoever he may be. I've come round to that way of thinking, after all I've been through. Retired on a nice little pension and settled, would you believe, in a small village just outside Jerusalem. You'd think I'd want to get away from that city, full of unrest and heaving with mischief as it is. But I'd better tell you who I am, and how I came to be here.

Gaius Diderus Lucius at your service, that's me. Roman soldier, retired. Never rose above the ranks, never wanted to. Served out my time, received the citizenship from a not-too-thankful Caesar and stayed put in my last assignment place.

What a place! What a time to be here! Uprisings and rebellions and crucifixions. I served only twelve years, and they were probably the worst of my services. I reckon it won't be long before the Emperor Vespasian puts these people down once and for all, and razes the city to the ground. Glad I'm well out of it.

I'd been serving with centurion Gallus, as his personal body servant. We got on well; he was a good man to serve. He got on well with the community too, rebuilt their meeting place, synagogue they call it. I think he valued me. Well, I remember one time when I had the sweating sickness, and Gallus went off to find the Galilean healer to ask him to heal me. Jesus, his name was. Shan't forget him in a hurry. There I was tossing and turning, with my body feeling as though it was burning up and my brain going every which way in my head, when suddenly, about mid-day, it all stopped. Like a cool breeze over me and a deep sleep. Got up after that and got on with work. Gallus said it all happened just the time when he spoke to the healer.

Jesus-bar-Joseph. Never forget that name. Never will. If it really had worked out as Gallus said, well I owe him my life.

Came across him again, later. At a time I remember most: one Passover time, one of their religious festivals. The city overcrowded with excitable folk.

I'd been transferred from Gallus' command to guard duty in the city, lots of troops drafted in at Passover for obvious reasons. This one time, crowds coming to Pilate demanding the end of a trouble-maker. Astonishing really, they blackmailed Pilate into doing what they wanted: to get rid of this one particular man. A dangerous criminal? Security threat? You'll be surprised when I tell you who it was. A Galilean. Named Jesus. Jesus-bar-Joseph. Couldn't be the same one I thought, must be lots with that name. But, I heard it was the same man. I'd of course never met him, Gallus would have known, but he was still back in Galilee. Chap I served under now – Longinus – he was put in charge of executing the three fellows condemned, this Jesus chap being one of them.

I hate doing crucifixions. Pah! Nasty, messy business. And this one I'd have done anything to avoid. But when you're in the Roman army, you do as you're told, no question. The others made a mock of it, and him. Put that stupid cloak on him and thorny crown; produced their dice; gambled for his robe; joined in the catcalls. I just watched.

Was this the man who had healed me two, three years ago now? If it was, he'd done a lot of healing people apparently, curing blindness, lameness, even curing leprosy they said. So what was he doing here, strung up on one of our crosses? Longinus had his doubts about him too.

I fetched him wine vinegar. Helps to dull the pain. Watched a while. Spooky time it was with the light fading at mid-day like it was evening. He didn't take long to die. Helped take him down. Important chap came for the body.

Ah yes! The body! Well, the Jewish authorities weren't satisfied with having him crucified, dead and buried. They wanted a guard put on the tomb. In case he escaped or something? Did they think we Roman soldiers couldn't do our job properly? No-one, but no-one, survives our crucifixions. When we took him down he was well and truly dead. Get it? D.E.A.D, dead.

Anyway, I got assigned guard duty over that tomb. Thought it was a cushy number. Who'd think his followers would steal a body? Daft thing to think. Slunk off and gone to ground they had and don't blame them either. No, I looked forward to a bit of shut-eye that night.

But – and here's where I'm going to tell you what you won't believe. I couldn't sleep a wink. No-one, absolutely no-one came to the tomb that night. The air was full of stirrings, rustlings, whisperings that weren't animals or wind or night birds. Or the chap's followers. There was a strange light over that tomb, as though morning had come too early, just as night had come too early the day before. And we all felt the fear. The earth shaking and rumbling as that huge stone, with our seal still intact on it, shivered and rolled away.

Don't remember much after that. Except there were comings and goings of women. I looked inside the cave at one point. No body. That meant huge trouble for us! We'd been set to guard a body and we'd lost it. Don't laugh!

I know what I believe. I know, and have told what I know, that here was a man who was also a god. Or rather, Son of God. And death could not hold him, however many stones were piled up in front of his tomb.

He lives – still.

He lives – now.

Chapter 15
AN ORDINARY WOMAN

Then the apostles went back to Jerusalem from the Mount of Olives… they gathered frequently to pray as a group, together with the women …
When the day of Pentecost came, all the believers were gathered together in one place …
Acts 1: 12, 14; Acts 2: 1

Deborah would not describe herself as anything but ordinary. Middle-aged, a bit dumpy, hair going grey. She had been married to Simeon-bar-Josiah, a good man, equally ordinary, for nearly thirty years; borne him four children, all married, bringing up their own families and doing nicely thank you (well, with one exception). Together Deborah and Simeon worked their small farm, lived an ordinary life, both of them quiet, unobtrusive, shy.

You wouldn't think a small farm on the outskirts of the small village of Bethany, itself on the outskirts of Jerusalem would be a suitable place for huge, momentous, extra-ordinary happenings. But so it was.

The farm was bordered by rocky outcrops and part of Simeon's job was to keep the caves hidden within these rocks clean and swept, for they were burial caves. Part of Deborah's work was weaving the long strips of cloth used to wrap the bodies; tending the herb garden and drying the herbs used to layer the wrappings. They were both there, of course, at the burial of Lazarus, brother to Martha and Mary. Martha and Deborah were two of a kind: practical, hard-working, sensible women; Mary was made of different stuff, reflective, a dreamer. And it was Mary who had introduced Jesus to the small village of Bethany. Deborah wasn't at all sure what to make of him.

But of course they were there, she and Simeon, when Jesus called Lazarus back from the dead. As he came out, shuffling, pale, blinking in the daylight, Deborah though she would die of fright and take his place in the dark cave!

The weeks and months that followed seemed to Deborah, struggling to maintain her ordinary life, to be a blur of momentous events. Their youngest son, Johann, instead of doing his work on the farm, took himself off to Jerusalem to follow this man Jesus.

'He's not only a prophet,' Johann declared, 'he's the Messiah! He'll bring the sovereignty back to Israel! He'll defeat the Romans!'

Deborah kept her doubts to herself on that one.

But it wasn't long before Johann came back with his tail between his legs. And a story of Jesus' horrific death on a Roman cross, and an end to all their hopes. An end to the dreams young Johann had nursed of a free Israel, free from Roman occupation.

But then came the strange story of Jesus returning from death (like Lazarus? thought Deborah to herself); appearing to his friends. The news trickled down to the good folk of Bethany; was whispered behind closed doors, talked over, doubted. In spite of herself, Deborah was stirred, amazed, doubting but desperately wanting to believe. So much so, that when Mary came, with no doubts at all in her mind, and asked if Deborah would go to Jerusalem with her to join the disciples at the feast of Pentecost, she agreed almost without thinking.

'I can always take some fleeces to sell in the market,' she excused her decision to Simeon.

He was unsure about letting her go, but knew she would be with Mary and Martha, Lazarus as well. She would be safe, he thought.

He did not know she would be become part of astonishing events that were far from safe! Nor how she, Deborah, a very ordinary woman, would be caught up in wind and fire; inspired by the words of Peter the apostle, and would find herself babbling to complete strangers all she knew of Jesus of Nazareth: who he was, what he had done, what he had taught, what he stood for.

The Spirit was poured out on her: an ordinary daughter of Israel, a good wife and mother, so that when she came back to Bethany, back to her daily tasks, she went about them with a spring in her step. And as she did so, she told all who would listen this wonderful, incredible story. It did not stop there, the wonder continued.

Deborah, the quiet, unobtrusive, shy, shared the good news with anyone and everyone: at home, at the well, in the market place.

So that in her small village, the good news began to spread – and went on spreading.

All over the world.

Chapter 16
FAMILY-BAR-JOSEPH

'I came to set sons against their fathers, daughters against their mothers ... a man's worst enemy will be the members of his own family.'
Matthew 10: 35 – 36; (Luke 12: 51 – 53; 14: 26 - 27)

My Aunt Salome and I have both told our family story elsewhere ('Daughters of the Way' Rosi MorganBarry, 161 Feather Books Poetry Series) how as a family we were split apart and then came together in unexpected ways. But some stories can bear re-telling, indeed need to be told more than once for folk to find the whole truth in them. First – here is Aunt's story, as she told it to Dr Luke:

'Come in, come in, I know who you are, my sister Mary told me. You're the Greek doctor, friend of Saul, or Paul as he's known now. You want to write about our Jesus-bar-Joseph. Well, I knew him all his life. But first things first, water for your feet and wine for thirst, and then to share a meal with us. Not much, bread fresh from the oven, a little goat's cheese and olives. Will it do?

Did Mary tell you of the family furore? It was all to do with James, and Joseph. No, not my James, nor yet the other Mary's – wait: I'd better sort out for you our family's complications.

On our side, there's me, the elder, Salome. My husband's name was Zebedee, God rest him. We had eight sons; the two eldest quick-tempered, and loud, just like their father. Jesus nicknamed them, sons of thunder. They were James and John. After them, six others! And then, came late to bless us, daughter Sara. Then there's my sister Mary, married to Joseph-bar-Jacob, the carpenter, widowed now long since, and she had Jesus, James and Joseph-junior (we called him Jo), Simon, Judas, and the girls Miriam and then Salome, named after me. Now, Joseph's brother, he was called Clopas, though some named him Alphaeus, being the first-born; he married the other Mary and they had sons: James, nicknamed the smaller, and Joses. Hope you've got all that. Don't worry if not; we're a complicated family.

Were we a close-knit family? Now there's a question! We got on well enough at weddings and funerals. But it was at my daughter's wedding that the rift truly started. We found a good man for her – Joachim, a wine merchant of Cana in Galilee. All Cana turned out for the feasting, knowing the wine would flow, so much so, they ran out! Mary told Jesus of it; she was anxious, but Jesus said:

'That's not our business, mother.'

Nonetheless, he put things right. Do you know the story? His brothers, James and Jo, were furious, thinking he courted glory with some cheap trick. Cheap? That wine was top grade quality! I've never drunk any better!

Not long after that, he went away, Jesus I mean, preaching and healing. And my boys went haring after him, as did little James. All the other men, brothers and cousins, uncles and in-laws, even my good husband, they all thought he was mad, and bent on trouble. Me? What did I think? If you had asked me that some years ago I would have said the same, mad, even devil-possessed. But yet, they told us of such wonders!

Did you know, when he came back to Nazareth, Jesus I mean, after he'd been away out in the desert somewhere, he read the lesson in the synagogue: Isaiah's words about the blind recovering their sight, and good news brought to the poor, the captives, people in distress. What's mad in that? But there was more, of course there was. He got himself on the wrong side of authority and that – as Zebedee used to say – is setting sparks to tinder. He said himself, Jesus that is, that he had come to bring fire to the earth, and how he wanted it kindled! And he also said he would divide families:

father against son, mother against daughter. How true that was! It happened to us.

I think now, looking back, he was a man of passion, and roused passions for, or against.

And those who were against, had power of death for him. I was there, when the death they had devised caught up with him. A dreadful death; a dreadful time. We were all shocked. I went to comfort my poor sister, who had stayed to watch. How she had the courage I shall never know. Together with the other women, we planned his burial.

But then, our spices of death were scattered to the winds! Instead we witnessed a morning of such joy, I cannot, even now, speak clearly of it. I could not then, although I tried to tell, but the men, lordly in their superiority, refused to believe us.

More wine? And try my raisin cakes, the best in Capernaum they say. And you must rest. Tomorrow, talk to my niece, my namesake. Let her tell you what she knows.'

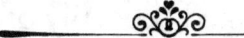

'Salome two they call me, named for my aunt. I've talked before about when I was little and wanted so much to read and write like the boys, and how my brother Jesus, instead of laughing and teasing, said if I could learn, it would be a gift from God. And one day it might be useful. I did learn, and have since written our family story. Our Rabbi was kind enough to give me parchment and ink, and I have it here, Dr Luke, please take it for your use. I know you want to write your own story about Jesus, and about our family.

Have you talked to mother? She puts herself down, does mother. Just an ordinary country girl, she'll say. And yet, she had such strength! She brought up the seven of us, and kept us all clean and well-fed, sometimes on little money when trade was bad and father's handiwork didn't fetch the price it should. That's when he'd take the job he hated: making crosses for Roman crucifixions. 'Waste of a tree', he'd mutter, 'God didn't make this wood, full of life and beauty, to be an instrument of blood'.

Jesus, working with him, would shake his head, and say nothing.

When father died, mother wept for days, but never stopped her work. She baked the daily bread, cooked dinner, washed and mended clothes, tended the herb patch, milked the goat, who turned a startled head as tears ran down her flanks. We girls helped as we always had, but keeping busy was the only way mother could cope.

Jesus took over as head of the household and for several years ran the carpenter's shop, until such time as he went away, took up his mission. Both James and Joseph-junior were working the shop then, but they strongly resented his going. And it was James who declared him mad, wanted him put away, said he was a disgrace to the family. He was implacable, was James, and dragged Simon and Joseph with him. Miriam too. But mother, Jude and I, we held our peace.

Did Aunt tell you of that dreadful day when Jesus came back to Capernaum? How James insisted we all went to hear him preach? Except James wouldn't listen, stayed outside, and sent a message saying we were there, wanting to talk to him. And Jesus said:

'Who is my mother? Who are my brothers? All you, who do the will of Father God. You are my mother, sisters, brothers!'

Well! You can imagine. James was beside himself. Even Jude was puzzled and angry. But mother astounded us all.

'He's right,' she said, 'his family are all those who support his work. Not those of us who set themselves against'.

James shut up like a trap and from that day on refused to speak of Jesus.

Until the end. Until after the end. Mother and I were there when Jesus died. Don't ask, I can't tell you what it was like. All I could think about were father's words:

'No tree should be an instrument of blood'.

But afterwards, more miracles than ever I'd have thought were possible. Even for God! James, you see was appalled at Jesus' death. You would have thought he'd shrug and say it served him right, but no! The day our brother died, James took a vow of prayer and fasting, which he said he'd keep till he met Jesus face to face once more. At the last day.

He came one Sabbath evening. We were at supper. Mother had lit the candles, said the prayer to bring the Sabbath in, called us to dinner. And Jesus came. Looking just as he'd always looked, serene and laughing. Except his hands and head were dark with bruising. He shared the meal with us, talked of the Scriptures, he and James matching quotations, as they had always done.

And afterwards, they went together, out into the starlight. Quietly, companionably.

As brothers should

www.ingramcontent.com/pod-product-compliance
Lightning Source LLC
Chambersburg PA
CBHW071535080526
44588CB00011B/1678